Questions of Science and Faith

Questions of Science and Faith

J. N. Hawthorne

Inter-Varsity Press

© INTER-VARSITY PRESS, LONDON

Inter-Varsity Fellowship
39 Bedford Square
London WC1B 3EY

First published in this edition April 1972

ISBN 0 85110 450 9

Printed in Great Britain by
Richard Clay (The Chaucer Press), Ltd.,
Bungay, Suffolk

Contents

Introduction

A book on science and Christianity must attempt to cover a good many fields of knowledge. I can't claim to be an authority on all of them.

Theologians will probably smile at my simple approach to their subject! Science itself is so specialized today that a biochemist's view of physics or anthropology may be most inadequate. I hope it isn't actually misleading! So it ought perhaps to be said that the views expressed in this book are personal opinion and in no way represent an official outlook for which the publishers are to be held responsible.

The text and layout have been extensively revised for this new edition and I am indebted to Miss Clare Richards of Inter-Varsity Press for thus producing a more readable book. My thanks are also due to my wife and to Dr Philip Duke for helpful criticism of the manuscript in its early stages.

If dedications hadn't been unsuitable in a small book of this sort, I should have inscribed it to one of my school-masters, Mr F. T. Johns, who first showed me that science alone was not enough.

J.N.H.

1 Misunderstanding

It is a capital mistake to theorize
before one has data —
Sherlock Holmes.

'You can't believe that sort of stuff now – science has disproved all that. . . .' 'Of course science contradicts Christianity. . . .' How often you hear things like that said nowadays!

Or, as a schoolboy put it, 'God created the animals, but the earth was scientifically formed.' For him, science was able to create things. To some extent at least it had replaced God.

Why do people assume there's a *conflict* between science and Christian faith? How has science come to *replace* God? There are a number of reasons.

Scientists have made staggering achievements in the last 100 years.

Men have walked on the moon. Electronics, with its television and computers, has mushroomed. Test-tube babies may be on the way.

It isn't surprising that the scientist is thought of as the wise man of today. His opinion is sought on everything from morality to toothpaste. Christianity on the other hand doesn't seem relevant to modern life.

9

Science is given more importance in our schools than religion.

Science is a vital subject. Religious education is often an extra, fitting in where it can, or it may not be part of the school syllabus at all. Few people take it as an exam subject while many take science. No wonder it seems unimportant.

Usually people who specialize in science do it at the expense of subjects such as RE and history. So it isn't surprising that they have a one-sided outlook. Only too often they see reality as being no more than scientific 'facts'. Other kinds of knowledge don't count.

But Christianity involves quite a different way of thinking. It is concerned with man's whole way of life. It doesn't just involve the mind, but the will: Christianity claims man's obedience.

The church itself has been at fault.

It has often failed to present Christianity in a simple, direct way. The 'good news' which is quite clear in the New Testament has been so obscured by out-of-date language and technical jargon that the ordinary person can't understand it.

There have been some unfortunate incidents in the past, too, which help to make people uneasy about science and Christianity.

In the seventeenth century Galileo was in trouble with the church for saying the earth moved round the sun. Kepler and Copernicus were unpopular for the same reason. The theologians of the time said the earth was the centre of all things, and everything revolved round it. They didn't get their ideas from the Bible, but from the Greek philosophers.

The Bible doesn't teach this or any other theory about the solar system. It certainly talks of the sun moving in the sky, but this is because it was written for ordinary people, and that's how it looks! No-one argues about the use of the word 'sunrise' today, although we know it is more accurate to speak of the earth rotating.

Three centuries later, at a meeting of the British Association in 1860, Bishop Samuel Wilberforce attacked Darwin's theory of evolution on the grounds that it contradicted the Bible. He ended a long speech by light-heartedly asking T. H. Huxley, who was presenting Darwin's views, whether he was related to a monkey through his grandfather or his grandmother. Huxley accused the bishop of being opposed to any form of open inquiry. A lot of ill-feeling resulted from the encounter which even now has not entirely disappeared.

In fact the Bible does not aim to give us a scientific theory of man's origin, as chapter 6 will show.

It has been suggested that pride may have made the bishop reluctant to believe that he had animal forebears: he couldn't face a monkey in his family tree! But the Bible talks of man being formed from the 'dust of the ground', an idea much more humbling than those of Darwin.

Science appears to have made some parts of the Bible untrue or impossible.

Was the world really made in six days?

Was Jonah really swallowed by a fish?

Was Lazarus really brought back from the dead?

Some people say that these and other things like them are just fanciful additions to the original texts. But they can't be dismissed lightly, for two reasons:

1. *We have better early manuscripts today than ever before, and these 'oddities' are still in them.*

2. *If they are removed, we lose essential parts of the narrative.*

In any case, it is neither scholarly nor scientific to edit the sources to suit one's own views. And if we do, how do we know where to stop? If we take away all the 'unusual' parts, the remainder will hardly be worth reading.

Some writers have used the findings of science to create their own philosophies of life, and advertise them as a substitute for Christianity.

These amateur philosophers tell us, often in the name of science, to get rid of old superstitions and face life in an adult way. If we apply the principles of science properly, we will create a happy world, they say.

The Bible isn't so naive. Its message is based on the fact that something is fundamentally wrong with the human race. This view fits the facts of history.

But the Bible gives a remedy too. The following chapters will consider whether there are any scientific reasons for mistrusting it.

2 Science

This knight was indeed a valiant
gentleman; but not a little given to
romance, when he spoke of himself –
John Evelyn.

We saw in the last chapter that people today think that
science gives all the answers. 'Scientific truth', they say, is
the only solid 'factual' truth available.

Before we go any further, we need to decide just what
science can and cannot do. Can science really give us a
'complete' view of the world, for instance?

Science is only one form of knowledge.

In fact the word 'science' originally meant 'knowledge'.
So any system of knowledge is strictly a 'science'. The
different 'sciences' are distinguished by the data they use and
the methods by which they arrive at their conclusions.

The 'science' of mathematics is a system of knowledge
built up by logical reasoning from self-evident truths. The
'science' of theology is derived in the same way from the
information in the Bible.

The subjects coming under the popular meaning of the
word 'science' are the experimental sciences – physics,
chemistry, biology, etc. – which depend on observation and
experiment. After a large number of observations have been

made on a particular subject or working theory, the results are studied and any regularities noted. These regularities form the basis of general laws. This method of reasoning is known as 'the scientific method'.

The 'scientific method' isn't always the best method of description.

Take the example of the blue sky. The scientist might describe it by talking of the scattering of light waves by atmospheric dust. This is a complete scientific description, but it is somehow still empty: it is divorced from what we actually see. A poet would give a totally different description which, again, would be complete in its own way, but would still not be the full account.

Science has shown that it doesn't give all the answers.

The Victorians used to think that science would soon tell them all there was to know about the universe. If we fully knew the positions and movements of the world's atoms at a given moment, they said, the whole future could be predicted.

But their optimism turned out to be ill-founded. At the beginning of this century an extraordinary change took place in physics, the fundamental experimental science.

It was caused by the arrival of quantum theory and relativity. In the words of Stephen Leacock: 'It was Einstein who caused the real trouble. He announced in 1905 that there was no such thing as absolute rest. After that there never was.'

We can't go into the subject deeply here, but one or two brief examples will show how great the change was.

1. *Atoms and electrons*. The old view of atoms was that they behaved like elastic billiard balls and were indivisible. We now know they are more like miniature solar systems with a central, positively-charged nucleus surrounded by spinning electrons. Much of the atom seems to be empty space.

The exact nature of electrons and other sub-atomic particles isn't understood. In some experiments the electron behaves as if it were a minute particle, in others as if it were energy in the form of waves. Its behaviour can be expressed in mathematical equations, but it is difficult actually to picture the electron.

A further difficulty has been summarized by Heisenberg, in his famous Uncertainty Principle (more about this in chapter 5). It is that our very observations affect the electron so that it can't be observed with precision at all. The observations alter the electron's speed or position so that we can know only a certain amount about it at any instant in time.

The Uncertainty Principle supplies a full stop which the Victorians would never have dreamed of!

2. *Light*. The Victorian theory of light was that it travelled as waves through a sort of universal sea, the 'ether'.

But this explanation no longer satisfies us. The nature of light remains a mystery. Some experiments 'prove' that it consists of a stream of photons, 'packets' of energy. Other equally reliable experiments show that it travels in waves. Again, what we know about light may be summed up in a mathematical equation, but this leaves the ordinary person with very little idea of the nature of light.

Scientists themselves are changing their views on the scope of science.

One result of these changes is that physicists themselves are rather humbler when they set out to describe ultimate truth! The 'new physics' leaves room for 'non-scientific' explanations. Sir James Jeans even found himself led to the idea of the universe as the work of a great 'Mathematician–Creator'.

Another result is the new emphasis on the observer in science. The old idea that science is solid, factual (or final) truth is gone. It is seen to consist of men's experience – gained in the laboratory by the use of the scientific method, but still experience.

So we can say that science is only one set of 'world-experiences'. Artists, prophets and poets give us other world-experiences equally worth while. One can't be played off against the other. They are complementary.

Science doesn't ask all the questions. It asks only specialized ones.

It tells us how things happen, but it doesn't tell us why. We may understand, for example, how the blood-sugar level is controlled, or the movements of the planets. But science never tells us why things are like this. Look at two examples.

1. If we ask why an apple falls to the ground when it is dropped, we are told: 'Because of the law of gravity.'

But this is no explanation. The law merely states what we have observed, though in a more general way: that there is an attraction between the apple and the ground. Admittedly, it gives a more precise description, telling how this attracting force depends on the masses of earth and apple and their distance apart.

We could find out even more along these lines, but just *why* it should happen is not for science to say. Science can give us the 'know-how', but it can't give us the 'know-why'. We are so used to 'gravity' that we fail to see how amazing it is that one body should pull on another when there is nothing between them to transmit the force.

2. To take a second example, think of a forest fire. You might ask why it was burning and get two equally true answers.

One might be: 'Because someone was careless enough to drop a match.' Another would be more involved, and might run: 'Because trees contain a great deal of carbon, an element which can undergo exothermic reaction with the oxygen of the air to give various gaseous products . . .' and so on.

Science could contribute only the second of these answers. Christianity, on the other hand, deals with more basic questions and uses language similar to that of the first answer.

The realm of science is different from that of the Bible.

Scientists ask a different sort of question, as we have seen. They are concerned with measurements, relations between things, mechanisms – the 'how' of the universe.

You can't get moral or aesthetic values from scientific data. Attempts have been made to base a code of ethics, a system of right and wrong, on the theory of evolution. Those actions which led to the survival of the race were said to be 'good' ones.

But this takes for granted that the survival of the human race is a good thing in itself. A disinterested Martian looking at the present international situation might consider that we have carried on quite long enough.

And if, as science assures us, the earth will one day be unable to support life, why bother to fight (or not fight) for a few years more or less?

The Bible gives us a real basis for our moral code. That is its realm: it is a book about right and wrong, about why we are here and why man, occasionally noble, has on the whole made such a mess of things.

Above all, it is a book about the One who formed and who sustains this extravagant and complicated universe.

But that is another chapter.

3 The Bible

If this plan and work of theirs is a
man-made thing, it will disappear;
but if it comes from God you cannot
possibly defeat them –
Acts 5:38.

The Bible is the world's best-selling book. Why should this
be so? Isn't it just one book among thousands?

Its own pages claim far more than that. . . .

The Bible claims to be inspired by God.

This is why it is referred to as the 'Word of God'. The
claim is that its writers were inspired in a special way, that
God spoke through them – not in any mechanical way but
through the obedience of their lives and minds. Their
thoughts were, in effect, His thoughts.

This isn't hard to believe when you look at the things they
foretold: the Messiah's birth, the fall of Jerusalem in AD 70,
the return to Palestine of the Jewish nation which has taken
place in our own day and so on. Some of these prophecies
were so detailed, and the events they foretold so unlikely
from a human point of view, that we can't take them simply
as lucky guesses.

The Bible claims to be unique.

If it is inspired, we can't judge it by comparing any other

book with it. It's no use comparing books of man's philosophy or science. If these find 'fault' with the Bible, how can we be sure that they aren't wrong?

You can't judge the Bible by methods of science either. Many of the facts in it about history or archaeology have been checked and found correct. This helps to make us more confident about some of what it says.

But other statements can't be checked like this. Science can't make judgments on moral questions. Who is to say that the Ten Commandments are right or wrong, for example?

If we look at other systems of morals, we find all kinds of different ideas, although some have certain points in common. How do we know which is right?

Human wisdom alone can't provide a convincing logical basis for any ethical system. At some point assumptions have to be made.

Christians make the assumption that men on their own can't find out God's point of view. He had to intervene in history to reveal it. The whole Bible shows that this intervention has happened.

How *can* you test the Bible, then?

If I want to decide whether or not to trust someone I know with one of my possessions, I shall want to get to know him better first. I might want to ask his friends if he is reliable. It's no good observing him as a scientist might – weighing him, analysing his brain, measuring his reflexes. The best experiment of all will be actually to trust him with something valuable, if I am brave enough.

In the same way the Bible can be tested only by reading it and seeing whether it rings true; whether its words speak to heart and conscience; best of all, whether its central character could be the Son of God. If the record about Jesus is true, the rest will soon fall into place.*

It is a matter of heart and will, not just the mind. 'Whoever is willing to do what God wants will *know* whether what

* See the section on 'The Claims of Christ' in John Stott's *Basic Christianity* (Inter-Varsity Press).

I teach comes from God or whether I speak on my own authority,' said Jesus. As with Christianity itself, we need to obey the Bible in faith before we can be sure about it.

The Bible doesn't claim to be a textbook of science.

This is something we usually overlook. Why should God reveal to us what we can find out for ourselves? And if He did, how could we understand it all? Imagine Moses trying to sort out the theory of relativity, or modern ideas on the chemistry of the cell nucleus. And imagine today's scientists presented with the results of AD 3000.

The Bible does say something in passing about nature. Often its writers are acute observers of nature, but they observe it with a poet's eye rather than a scientist's. It's not wise to read too much into these statements: as we should expect, they use the ideas of their time.

When they talk about 'the pillars of the earth' we don't have to conclude that the earth stands on pillars.

Although Isaiah speaks of 'the circle of the earth' it doesn't mean that he knew it was round. He also refers to 'the ends of the earth'!

All the same, biblical writers are remarkably free from fantastic theories about nature, of the sort that were common in the 'science' of many ancient peoples.

The account of the creation in Genesis, for example, has great simplicity and depth compared with the myths of Babylon or ancient Greece.

The many references to the stars in the Old Testament emphasize their immense number and huge distance from us, but don't go into theories about their movements, and whether gods and goddesses ride them around the sky!

Instead the Bible has more important things to tell us – about man's nature, his broken relationship with his Creator and God's way of putting this right.

It presents us with the essential facts about God and man.

But it doesn't give us a complete, water-tight philosophical system answering all possible questions.

There are many questions it doesn't set out to answer. But it also presents some truths which are too deep for us to understand.

Take the example of free will and predestination: if God is in control of everything, He knows first what choices we are going to make. So how can we say we are free to act as we like?

Some verses in the Bible seem to imply that a man is free to choose whether or not he becomes a Christian. Others suggest that it is God who makes the choice. It seems that we shall never be able to reconcile these views from our position inside time.*

(Strangely enough, science has this kind of dilemma too. The problem of the nature of light and of the electron, referred to in chapter 2, present a similar difficulty. A famous physicist once said that he believed in particles on Mondays, Wednesdays and Fridays, but waves on Tuesdays, Thursdays and Saturdays!)

The Bible's teaching is clear on all that we need to know, as long as we don't ignore any of its statements on a particular subject.

If we read it thinking only of science we gain very little; the authors had greater things in view than the study of nature. Their book is a plan to save the ship-wrecked human race, not a philosophical discussion.

The apostle Paul called it 'the sword of Spirit'. You can't use a sword from an armchair!

* There is a helpful passage on this subject near the end of *The Great Divorce* by C. S. Lewis (Geoffrey Bles).

4 Points of view

Soap and education are not as sudden
as massacre, but they are more
deadly in the long run –
Mark Twain.

Education does make a difference. If someone were taught only maths and science and kept away from all literature and poetry, he would have an unusual attitude to things.

He would probably describe a symphony in terms of frequencies, overtones and mathematical regularities. But this description would mean very little to someone who had never heard the music.

The ordinary person would perhaps compare the music to a sunset or a stormy sea, or joy, or sorrow. This might convey the sounds much better.

The 'scientific' description could in principle be complete in every detail: it could cover the whole symphony. So could any other sort of description be complete – in its own way.

The two descriptions seem to be contradictory, but they are complementary. In other words, both are needed to give a complete picture. Each gives different details, different points of view.

The difficulty starts when the man with one sort of training won't accept the other sorts of description, saying they are unimportant or even misleading. It is very easy to do this, especially for scientists.

If you watch a film with a keen photographer you will probably find that he misses a lot of the story because he has become so engrossed in the cameraman's technique. He sees the film from one point of view only.

So we must recognize that there are different points of view.

Let us look at some examples.

1. We could describe the crossing of the Red Sea by the Israelites, mentioned in Exodus, in terms of theology or of science.

The Bible says that 'the Lord drove the sea away all night with a strong east wind and turned the sea-bed into dry land. The waters were torn apart. . . .'

From the scientific point of view we might say that the crossing was made possible by 'natural causes' – a strong wind and possibly some sort of earthquake which changed the level of the sea-bed.

The 'miracle' comes in the timing of the event. The interesting thing is that the sea dried up just when the Jews wanted to get across. The Egyptians weren't so lucky.

Our one-track-mind scientist who has no other evidence than this can only say that it was an odd coincidence. The Christian sees God acting through nature.

These two views are complementary; one doesn't exclude the other. In fact, the writer of Exodus himself suggests both.

2. David, in Psalm 8, looks up at the night sky and sees 'thy heavens, the work of thy fingers, the moon and the stars set in their place by thee'. He emphasizes God's marvellous handiwork. The same scene could be described in a text-book of astronomy with no mention of the Creator.

There are two levels of meaning, for the psalmist and for the astronomer, but each is true.

3. A broken window and a small boy with a catapult will

23

get different reactions. To the scientist it might show that a projectile with a certain velocity had enough kinetic energy to shatter glass of such-and-such a thickness. To the person who owned the house with the broken window it would probably prove that boys of seven shouldn't be allowed to use catapults!

The same event is being looked at in two different ways.

Scientific terms can nearly always be used to describe something. But they aren't always appropriate.

There is a danger in using the scientific method. When anything has been described in scientific terms, we are inclined to say, 'This is the whole truth. No other description can add anything to this.'

Take some more examples.

1. Fear may be described in terms of physiology. We might hear someone talking of adrenalin secretion or of electrical impulses. We should then soon draw the conclusion that man is only a complicated chemical mechanism – a collection of atoms. He certainly is, but he isn't *merely* that; there are many more apt descriptions.

2. You could describe this page in terms of the numbers of different letters used and of how they are arranged. You could say how many times 'an' or 'ie' come, for example, or 's' before a space. But if that were *all* the meaning you found, the author would naturally be disappointed! It would show that you had no interest in the meaning of the words.

3. To say that this page is a sheet of cellulose with small black dots on it is helpful as far as it goes. But it would be more to the point to say that it is a book on science and faith. To say that it is *merely* a sheet of cellulose with small black marks on it is actually misleading, quite apart from being unkind!

'Merely' is a dangerous word, and an unscientific one, since it assumes that we 'know it all'.

This idea of complementary descriptions makes us think less of God as a 'God of the gaps'.

In the past people have tended to bring God in only where science failed. The most famous example is probably in the field of cosmology, the study of the origin of the universe.

Until the eighteenth century, people couldn't imagine how the universe could have come into being. So they attributed it to God's intervention.

Even Newton couldn't complete his system of mechanical causes and effects without bringing in angels or some sort of supernatural being to give a necessary push at some stage in the process.

Laplace thought that he had completed the system. Napoleon asked him where God came in the process. He replied, 'Sir, I have no need of that hypothesis.'

He wasn't making out a case for atheism, as he believed in God. He was simply stating the fact that God shouldn't be brought in here to fill a gap in our knowledge. The gap had now been filled.

In a similar way modern theories of cosmology, whether they involve a 'continuous creation' or an initial 'big bang', don't bring in the Creator. We will say more about this in chapter 6.

Theories about the origin of life are not so convincing. The less sophisticated Christian feels that God is still needed here. 'Suppose all the atoms are put together in the right way: it took God to put breath into them.'

Sometimes he even says he will give up his Christianity when life can be made in the test-tube, as though this were the only stronghold left for his faith.

The trouble with this sort of outlook is that the gaps are getting smaller. As the mechanisms of this or that process are discovered, God seems to be left with less and less territory.

The apostle Paul, quoting a Greek poet, was nearer the mark when he spoke of God in whom 'we live and move and are'.

Mechanisms aren't everything. Science tells us only how things work and how the universe might have come into existence. Knowing how doesn't make a thing happen. Even in the lab. someone has to do the experiment!

Science won't lead us to God, but it won't exclude Him either.

The Christian view of God isn't that He is a missing inventor who made everything and then left it as a man might leave a fully-wound clock.

God is immanent in His universe – He is in the midst of it always, but He is greater than it. In some ways the universe is like a thought in His mind.

To look at it another way, He is the Sustainer of the whole universe. 'He's got the whole world in His hand', as the Negro spiritual says.

The scientist would have nothing to study if that hand were removed.

5 Presuppositions

All things began in order, so shall
they end, and so shall they begin
again, according to the ordainer of
order and mystical mathematics of the
city of heaven —
Sir Thomas Browne.

We tend to think of the scientist as someone who deals with
concrete facts only. He never needs to use faith in his work,
we should say. But this is not so. Before he can even start his
work, the scientist needs to assume various things, make
certain presuppositions, which can never be proved by
reason alone. He has to put his faith in them.

**Scientists have to assume, or in other words have
faith, that the universe is an orderly place.**

To some, this may not seem to be a question of faith at all.
Haven't scientists *proved* that nature is uniform?

Actually they haven't proved it at all. If an apple has
fallen in a certain way ninety-nine times in the past, we
believe that it will do the same when dropped the hundredth
time. We can't prove this will be so. But we believe it will
happen, because we have faith that nature is uniform.

In fact, science has made progress only through the
irregularities in nature.

When a theory is first made, there usually turn out to be
facts that don't fit in, exceptions to the rule. These lead the

way to a better theory. The new theory will have to fit both the old facts and the odd new one. It will be a 'truer', more general theory.

Until they have a complete scientific description of everything in the universe, therefore, scientists can't be sure, from science itself, that some new irregularity won't undermine all their theories.

Some examples may make this clearer.

1. *Radioactive substances.* Scientists have discovered that each radioactive substance, such as radium, decays at a certain rate. They therefore know the particular life-span of each substance. Half the atoms in a quantity of radioactive phosphorus, for example, will decompose in fourteen days. This period of time is called the 'half-life'.

But this holds good only when we deal with large numbers of atoms, which we usually have to do, since atoms are so minute. Little is known about why one atom decomposes at a certain instant.

If we take just one atom of radiophosphorus, there is no way of telling when it will split up. It may happen in a second, an hour or ten years.

So what governs this? We could give three answers:

(*a*) that such decomposition obeys no law, i.e. it is random;

(*b*) that atoms have 'minds' of their own and decay when they want to;

(*c*) that there are laws governing all this, but scientific observations can't yet explain the factors involved.

Scientists usually take the third view. But this is not on the basis of science. It is because they assume that nature is uniform, working according to regular laws.

2. *Electrons.* We have mentioned the Heisenberg Uncertainty Principle before in connection with electrons (see page 15). This principle says that only a limited amount can be known about an electron at any one instant. We can know its position but not its speed, for instance.

This is a difficulty that can never be solved. It can be

illustrated in the following way. Suppose that our eyes were sensitive to radiation of very short wavelengths and that we could illuminate an electron with this under a special microscope.

To get more than just a blur, the wavelength of the 'light' would have to be very short indeed. But the shorter the wavelength, the greater the energy carried by the radiation. When the really short rays hit the electron, they would knock it aside, so that though we might see the electron clearly in theory, in practice it wouldn't be there! We should have to return to the long-wave radiation and say that the electron was somewhere inside the blur.

Some writers have deduced from this that an electron obeys no laws, but moves independently according to its own will! But this idea doesn't really fit in with the experiments. The Uncertainty Principle only states that the electron's movements can never be calculated *by man*, not that they are random.

Although scientists are unable to base their ideas about electrons on observation, their usual view is that we would find the electron is obeying laws of cause and effect, if we could see it! This view is based on faith in nature's uniformity.

Unless scientists assume that nature is basically the same all the time, they can't predict the future or estimate what happened in the past.

This has led to some interesting thoughts in cosmology, the study of the origin of the universe.

1. The idea that the universe is expanding, for example, suggests a definite beginning at some time in the past. The galaxies can't have been spreading out for ever.

2. Studies of radioactive minerals point to the same conclusion, as we shall see from chapter 6.

3. So do the discoveries about entropy. 'Entropy' may roughly be defined as the degree to which the energy of a

physical system is available for conversion into mechanical work. Entropy in the physical world is gradually increasing (i.e. the amount of available energy is decreasing).

This suggests that the universe had a definite beginning, as entropy cannot have been increasing indefinitely. But it also suggests an end of the universe, a 'heat death' when the universe has all its energy distributed evenly and therefore not available to do work or support life.

Scientists don't like these ideas of discontinuity in the universe, of a beginning and end. In order to avoid them both, they have suggested a universe which 'runs down' and 'winds up' again. In this way it would be able to continue indefinitely. But this would mean reversing the entropy law every few billion years, suggesting that entropy will start decreasing instead of increasing. So in order to defend uniformity, they have done away with it here!

We have shown that scientists need to assume that there is order in the universe. If it were chaotic, there could be no science.

So some philosophers have argued that the apparent order in the world of science simply comes from man's own liking for order. They say that science is just a mirror reflecting man's tidy mind. Outside it there is no orderliness at all.

But in saying this they are saying that there *is* order in one part of the universe – man's mind. If they agree to this, there is no reason why nature shouldn't be orderly too, unless completely separate forces have produced man's mind.

Another group of philosophers feel that the order scientists find in nature is no accident. To them it is evidence that an orderly mind designed nature, in the same way as an intricate machine reminds us of the engineers who made it. In fact, if the universe is some great accident without design or purpose, it is very surprising that it should have such complicated regularities. And the assumption that it is uniform becomes a very precarious one.

It is probably relevant that the scientific method, as we know it, began in the sixteenth century. The pioneers of the time – Francis Bacon, for example and, later, Boyle and Newton – believed that the universe was orderly and worth studying because they saw it as the work of an intelligent Creator.

It was their faith that made them want to study nature. This was all they needed to believe in a regular universe. With the psalmist they could say, 'The heavens tell out the glory of God, the vault of heaven reveals his handiwork.'

Scientists also assume that our senses and minds are trustworthy enough to give us a true picture of the universe. To put it another way, the order in the universe is of a kind which our human minds can grasp, and therefore come to understand and use.

How do scientists know that they give us truth about the universe? They may say that science presents a picture which 'works all right'. It enables them to build microscopes, or aeroplanes, or television sets. But this doesn't prove it is true: a system can work quite well and still be based on fallacies.

So scientists are not justified in claiming that scientific facts are the only truth we can know. They base their work on certain presuppositions, on things which are a matter of faith, not reason. So do workers in all other fields. And so do Christians.

If this were realized more often, people might be more willing to look into the basic assumptions of the Christian faith.

Unless scientists assume that our minds are reliable, they can't continue to study science.

As we have seen, some people say that you needn't assume that nature is uniform. You certainly can look for evidences of harmony and find them. But you can look for disorder and find that too, concluding that all is meaningless and that life first appeared on earth through an unlikely accident.

In this case, the same thing applies to man's mind – it is

just the result of irrational causes, not intelligent planning. But if this is so, why should our minds be reliable? How can we use them to deduce scientific or other truths?

This is how J. B. S. Haldane put it: 'If my mental processes are determined solely by the motions of atoms in my brain, I have no reason to suppose that my beliefs are true . . . hence I have no reason to suppose my brain to be composed of atoms.'*

C. S. Lewis, discussing the same thing, commented: 'Hence every theory which makes the human mind the result of irrational causes is inadmissible, for it would be proof that there are no such things as proofs, which is nonsense.'†

Some have tried to overcome the difficulty by comparing our brains with electronic computers. 'If these "brains" give the right answers,' they say, 'why worry that our own brains are not reliable? They are basically similar, just more complex.'

They may even go on to point out that computers prove there is no such thing as 'mind'. This 'materialist' view of life sees our brains as much the same as electronic 'brains'. Our brains just came into being from a chance collection of suitable atoms, on which irrational forces were working for an immense period of time.

In fact the comparison of our brains with computers suggests the opposite. No one thinks that computers just happened by chance. They are made by men who understand mathematics. They are made to give the right answers.

Presumably it is quite easy to make computers which always give the wrong answers. A machine made by shuffling the parts together until they come into some working arrangement would probably be one of them!

If our minds are to be trusted, it is better to think of them as having been designed by someone who knew the right answers. This is what Christians believe.

* J. B. S. Haldane, *Possible Worlds* (Harper).
† C. S. Lewis, *Miracles* (Geoffrey Bles).

So when people talk about 'the facts of science', we need to remember the assumptions that scientists make.

Like the Christian, the scientist uses faith.

Has he any better grounds for doing so than the Christian?

There are as many Christians who are scientists as there are Christians who are greengrocers or garage mechanics. They believe that scientists' assumptions are well grounded.

They would expect nature to be orderly because they know its Creator dislikes chaos. They also believe that human minds made by a God of truth should be trustworthy.

They are the true heirs of Galileo and Newton.

They have better grounds for their assumptions than their agnostic colleagues!

6 In the beginning

The poor world is almost six
thousand years old —
Shakespeare, *As You Like It.*

Just how far can we expect to get scientific information from
the Bible?

In Shakespeare's day, Archbishop James Ussher used the
Bible to work out the exact year in which the world began.
He made it 4004 BC.

John Lightfoot, a Cambridge scholar, went even further.
He announced that the creation took place during the week
18–24 October, 4004 BC. He worked out that Adam was made
at 9 a.m. on 23 October!

We're so used to millions and billions today that mere
thousands seem insignificant. The people in Shakespeare's
time probably thought 4,000 years was quite a generous
allowance for the earth's age.

But is it right to use the Bible in this way? Genesis speaks
of God creating the world in six days, for example. Are we
to take the word 'day' literally?

Some people say that 'six days' really means six lengthy
periods of time. Others would object that this goes against
the Bible's authority. We ought to take every word literally.

When reading the descriptions in the Bible, we need to remember certain things.

Any translation reflects the ideas of its translators to a certain extent, so we must be careful not to read too much into the actual words of any one translation.

This is particularly the case if it is an old translation, such as the Authorized Version. Some words have changed their meanings completely over the centuries. It's no use taking a word in its modern sense if it meant something quite different when the translation was written!

In any case, when the Bible was written in its original languages, some of the words used didn't have the exact scientific meaning that they have today.

Take the word 'day', for example. In the Hebrew, this is sometimes used to mean a period of twenty-four hours, or it can mean a much longer period, or an indefinite time.

Or there's the famous 'whale' that swallowed Jonah. The Authorized Version calls it a 'great fish' in the Old Testament (Jonah 1:17) and a 'whale' where it comes in the New (Matthew 12:40). The same Hebrew word is also translated 'dragon' or 'serpent' elsewhere in the Authorized Version of the Old Testament.

But we can't tell exactly which creature is being referred to. Our biological classification of living things wasn't started until about 2,000 years after the book of Jonah. Without a full description of its anatomy, no precise name can be given to Jonah's fish.

So one thing we need to do is make sure we are using the best, up-to-date translation that scholars have produced! Although we shouldn't read too much into our translations, that doesn't mean we can neglect any of the words in the Bible. God's meaning depends on them.

When we read the Bible, we should be aware of the type of writing we are reading: is it history or poetry, for example?

Some of the Bible contains reports of historical events, sometimes giving eye-witness accounts.

Other parts use poetic expressions – for example, 'the mountains skipped like rams': this is a poetic form of expression, not a scientific description of earthquakes.

It is usually possible to tell what is history and what is poetry, but in some places in Genesis it is extremely difficult to be certain how far the sense is literal and how far symbolic.

But one thing is clear: whether or not the details are symbolic, the disobedience of the first man and woman is the central fact.

To some people, the phrase 'the tree of the knowledge of good and evil' suggests that their disobedience involved more than taking fruit from a tree. Certainly 'Adam's apple' doesn't appear in Genesis. But while the tree could be symbolic, there's no such thing as symbolic disobedience!

Where 'scientific' matters are touched on, each writer of the Bible used the ideas of his own day so that he could be understood.

The writer of Genesis, normally thought to have been Moses, probably collected together many ancient records of Jewish history to cover events long before his own lifetime. Some of these may have been very old indeed, possibly written on clay tablets or not written at all. The first few chapters of Genesis probably represent the word's oldest records.

The people who compiled these records were chiefly concerned with Jewish history and God's relations with His chosen people. At that time the Jews had no formal study called 'science'. So in the modern sense, there is no science in Genesis.

It is true that the writers are sometimes inspired to record things which seem to be far ahead of their times. But this doesn't mean they understood the implications of what they wrote. The laws of hygiene in Leviticus, for example, might have been written by someone who understood all about infection caused by bacteria!

So the early chapters of Genesis set out to put over two central facts: (1) that God created everything and (2) that the first man and woman disobeyed Him, bringing evil into the world.

The Jewish account is quite different from the other early creation stories. In the Babylonian account, for example, there are grotesque and often ridiculous narratives, and a whole lot of gods are involved.

This sort of thing might have crept into Genesis if the writer had given his imagination free play. But its simple dignity and belief in one God are marks of more than human wisdom in its writer.

Today the statement 'In the beginning God created the heavens and the earth' sums up the cosmologists' theories just as well as it did in Kepler's time, or even in the days of Moses.

Modern science points to a beginning of the universe, as we saw in chapter 5.

The argument from the increase of entropy has already been mentioned. We can easily show that the world's oceans aren't infinitely old. The rivers of the world are steadily adding sodium salts to sea water at a rate that can be measured. In spite of this, only a limited amount of salt is found in the oceans.

Scientists can also date the beginning of the universe, within certain limits.

1. *Cooling of the earth*. An early attempt was made by William Kelvin. He assumed that the earth was originally molten. By estimating the rate at which it cooled and the amount of solid crust at that time, he worked out the earth's age at about thirty million years. We know now that that

figure is much too low. Today estimates are between three and five billion years.*

2. *Movement of stars.* Astronomers observing the relative movements of double and triple stars and galaxies conclude that these couldn't have existed longer than several billion years.

3. *Chemical elements.* The age of the chemical elements can also be calculated from the so-called 'geological clock'.

As mentioned in chapter 5, radioactive elements decay at different rates, and so each has a characteristic 'half-life' (that is, the time it takes for it to be reduced by half). Such elements 'decay' by giving off charged particles or gamma rays, and thus turn into other elements, which may be stable or decay even further.

Certain rocks contain uranium and thorium, which finally decay to lead. While the rock was still molten, the products of radioactive decay (among them lead) would diffuse away from their place of origin. Once the material became solid, the lead would accumulate alongside uranium and thorium. From the amount of lead, the age of the rock can be found. No rocks seem to be older than two billion years, by this method.

We get an even more convincing agreement by considering the relative amounts of two uranium isotopes in minerals. These are uranium–235 and uranium–238.

Uranium–238 has a half-life of 4,500 million years. It doesn't seem to have decayed very much yet! But uranium–235 is 140 times less abundant than uranium–238, and has a half-life of 500 million years.

So if it is halved in 500 million years it will have taken just over seven such periods to cut it down to 140th, that is 3,500 million years.†

This is the sort of date which science would give to Genesis 1:1.

---

* The American billion is used in this chapter – i.e. 1,000 million.
† $\frac{1}{2} \times \frac{1}{2} \times \frac{1}{2} \times \frac{1}{2} \times \frac{1}{2} \times \frac{1}{2} \times \frac{1}{2} = \frac{1}{128}$

Today's scientists are also trying to answer the question, 'How did the universe begin?'

Their studies usually point to a definite beginning, but none supplies a very adequate explanation of it. And they can't answer the question, 'Where did the matter in the universe come from?'

Hoyle's theory of 'continuous creation' is something of an exception. According to this Cambridge astronomer, the matter of the universe is being created all the time, at an immeasurably slow (though calculable) rate.

At the same time, the universe is expanding. If it weren't, space would come to contain more and more matter! So Hoyle maintains that the universe is infinitely old, although our own galaxy goes back only 5,000 million years.

Hoyle's actual words on the origin of matter are: '. . . it does not come from anywhere. Material simply appears – it is created.'*

One of chemistry's fundamental laws fifty years ago was the law of the conservation of matter. This stated that matter could not be created or destroyed in a chemical reaction.

Physicists have changed that in the last few decades. Einstein's famous equation $E = mC^2$ summarizes the tremendous fact that matter can be 'destroyed' or converted into an enormous amount of energy. In fact, we think of matter and energy today as two forms of the same thing. The old law has been rewritten as the law of the conservation of mass-energy.

All the same, Hoyle's theory defies this law, though in a very gentle way, since the matter in his universe is created so slowly. But in fairness it should be mentioned that it doesn't violate the conservation law as far as *experiments* show. The law hasn't been tested to an accuracy comparable with Hoyle's rate of creation.

But other cosmologies defy the law too, in a more dramatic way – for example, the theory that a 'cosmic explosion' was the beginning of things.

* See F. Hoyle, *The Nature of the Universe* (Blackwell), p. 105.

The 'expanding universe' has been referred to in chapter 5. It is widely held that the 'shift to the red' in the spectral lines from distant galaxies is caused by the rapid movement of these stars away from the earth.

These lines are produced by well-known chemical elements in the cooler gas within the galaxy. Their normal positions are known from the sun's spectrum. In the light from the distant galaxies they have a slightly longer wavelength than expected – in other words, they are moved to the red end of the spectrum.

Just as a train's whistle seems to change in pitch as it passes us at speed (the 'Doppler effect'), this wavelength change is thought to be caused by the star's rapid flight from us. Wherever we look this seems to be happening; the whole universe seems to be expanding.

The matter of the universe is now spread thinly through empty space. But some cosmologists believe it once formed a tremendously dense ball of material whose volume was only about 1,000 times that of the sun.

From the distance between galaxies and the speed at which they are separating, the time at which they began to separate may be calculated. Again, it proves to be a few billion years ago.

There is little in modern cosmology to contradict Genesis, and a good deal which fits in very well.

Someone might object: 'Even if you say God created everything, who created God? Surely you're only putting the difficulty one stage further away.'

According to the Bible, God is self-existent. That is, He never was created. But the criticism raises an important point.

The reason for summarizing a little of the recent scientific work in 'creation' isn't to show that Christianity has some easier or more plausible answer, or even that 'science supports the Bible'.

It is rather to show that science can't give an opinion as to

40

whether God arranged that 'cosmic explosion' or started the expansion of the universe in any way.

Questions of this sort must be answered from the data of revelation. They are beyond the terms of reference of science.

7 Life

Truth suffers more by the heat of its
defenders than from the arguments of
its opposers —
William Penn.

There was a time when scientists believed that life could
arise spontaneously from suitable mixtures of brewed hay
or old meat. Even in 1837 Andrew Cross claimed to produce
a new species of beetle by the electrolysis of certain solutions!

This idea of spontaneous generation – that life can come
from non-living matter – was very firmly rooted. Even when
Louis Pasteur's brilliant work demolished the myth there
was considerable opposition to him.

But many of the people who opposed Pasteur didn't do it
on scientific grounds. It was because Pasteur's ideas
wouldn't fit in with their own philosophy!

The idea of life arising 'naturally' from the dust and going
back to it again in an endless cycle seemed to fit in with
materialism, while Pasteur's ideas suggested to many the
intervention of a Creator.

Ernst Haeckel (1834–1919), for example, the German
biologist, claimed that spontaneous generation must be true,
not because it could be confirmed by experiment in the
laboratory, but because otherwise it would be necessary to
believe in a Creator.

Today materialists somehow feel that it would be a feather in their cap to show that life can arise by the operation of ordinary chemical laws. It probably isn't a coincidence that the first international symposium on the origin of life was held in Soviet Russia in 1957. Christians, on the other hand, have tended to line up with Pasteur.

But the important thing is to concentrate on the scientific facts and avoid unjustified leaps into philosophy! What exactly do science and the Bible say about life's origins? Can we believe both accounts?

The Bible tells us that a Designer was responsible for the appearance of the first life on earth, and for the sequence of changes that took place afterwards.

Genesis doesn't tell us whether life was formed by becoming gradually more complex, or whether the process was more sudden. Some people hold that God created all the different forms of life, whole, in an instant of time. But the six 'days' in the creation story suggest that there was a time sequence and that the simpler forms of life came first.

The Genesis account certainly isn't a scientific treatise. So it would be wrong to expect too much scientific detail from it.

From the scientific viewpoint, the appearance of the first germ of life in the sea or soil of the primitive earth is still such an improbable event that the word 'miraculous' could be applied to it. But of course scientists would be careful not to use the word, in case of misunderstanding!

The main scientific theory about the origin of life is the theory of evolution, first propounded by Darwin. He suggested that the different forms of life we now see in the world all arose by natural selection ('survival of the fittest') from a few simple living things.

This theory is still held by very many scientists today, with various modifications and in several forms. It is still a theory. There are facts which many scientists believe support

43

it. Other theories have been put forward, though few have been supported by professional biologists.

But most of the popularity of the theory of evolution is due to the very effective semi-popular accounts written at the end of the nineteenth century by evolutionary enthusiasts.

There are still many difficulties about the theory, and things that are not fully understood. So we shouldn't stop thinking critically about it just because it is a fashionable theory. There are a number of things to bear in mind.

'Evolution' can't cause anything. Like 'gravity', it is only a word to describe something scientists have observed.

So we can't argue that 'evolution' actually *caused* the first appearance of life and all the changes afterwards.

The theory of evolution refers to the scientific realm only, to physical origins. Some people have extended it to apply to man's moral development.

They talk of 'man's rise from savagery', 'the moral evolution of the human race', etc. But history shows that men are just as good and bad now as they have been for the last few thousand years.

There has been *technical* progress, of course, but this has only increased our capacity to do good *and* evil. George Bernard Shaw remarked that our advances in medicine are toys compared with our battleships!

Darwin's original theory didn't actually account for the origin of life. It assumed the existence in the first place of a few simple living creatures.

But today the word 'evolution' is used popularly to cover the means by which life first appeared as well as the later changes. This confuses several different issues.

We don't actually know anything of the way in which life first arose – unless wild speculation can be called knowledge.

If the first protein was formed by a chance alignment of amino-acids, it is difficult to see how it could be built up into one large molecule without some sort of 'template', or pattern, to hold the amino-acids in the right relative positions. J. D. Bernal has suggested that certain clays might have served this purpose.

Another problem is that proteins are very sensitive to acid conditions. They can easily be 'denatured', or made inactive from a biological point of view, by other organic compounds and metallic salts. But the same mechanisms which produced amino-acids would also produce many of these destructive compounds, in even greater quantity – there are roughly twenty amino-acids but thousands of other organic chemicals of about the same molecular size.

So the first protein would have to be protected from these compounds – another difficult problem.*

There are gaps in the fossil record, particularly between the highest animals and man. This would argue against a continuous process of evolution.

It isn't easy to see how the first stages in the development of certain organs could be of 'survival value'. It's even more difficult to imagine mutations which could have given rise to the organs in one generation!

Evolution remains a hypothesis, the best hypothesis so far advanced in the opinion of most biologists. But that doesn't mean that it can be used as a basis for being dogmatic where there is no scientific evidence.

In its ideas of life becoming continually more complex, the theory of evolution seems to contradict the second law of thermodynamics.

This law sums up observations that there is a decrease of orderliness in all closed systems as time goes by. Left to themselves, atoms arranged in an orderly way became

* Some of these problems are discussed in the final chapter of *Enzymes* by M. Dixon and E. C. Webb (Longmans).

chaotic. Disorderly atoms certainly don't grow into living cells!

In fairness, we should mention an attempt to solve this difficulty. It is that, although in the whole solar system there is an over-all decrease of order, certain parts of it may be increasing their orderliness at the expense of others.

For instance, the sun loses vast amounts of energy and order so that a small planet, the earth, can afford the luxury of living things. Molecules such as chlorophyll are able to transfer light energy from the sun to living plants.

But this answer applies only when such molecules are already in existence. It isn't clear how the heat and light of the sun could help in the actual formation of these molecules or of the first molecules of protein and other complicated substances needed for life.

How do the early chapters of Genesis relate to theories of evolution? There are several views held today; we will consider two of them.

The first view states that development has taken place within certain large groups of living things, but it does not account for the whole biological picture as we see it.

In this view, the Creator intervened directly and brought the forebears of the main groups into being. This may or may not have taken place over a long period of time, depending on how the 'days' of Genesis 1 are interpreted.

In the same way, the first man and woman were the result of a special act of creation. When God is described in Genesis 2:7 as breathing into Adam's nostrils, He is giving him a quality of life not shared by the animals. In this sense, the first man is a 'living soul'.

Those holding this view explain the anatomical and biochemical similarities between man and the animals by emphasizing that one Creator made both. If all were to live together in one world, you would expect similarities of this sort. Some of these similarities, such as the ability to use the same basic food for energy, would certainly be useful.

According to the second view, man's similarities with the animals are because he is descended from them. God began and controlled the whole evolutionary process.

People holding this view believe that we shall eventually understand the physical mechanisms by which even man arose. But they admit that we are still a long way from doing this!

They would agree that there is still a great difference between man and the highest animals. To them the passage that speaks of man becoming a 'living soul' implies that only when a complex enough nervous system was available could the creature possessing it know God. He then became a 'living soul' capable of some kind of fellowship with the Creator.

On this view it is still possible that the first humans were two in number. But those who hold it admit that it is more likely that they would have been many. This makes two difficulties:

1. We should have to take it that Adam and Eve represented all the first humans. In that case the Genesis account would mean that *all* men and women disobeyed God in that first generation.

2. There are passages in the Bible, such as Romans 5:12–21, which contrast the *one* man through whom sin and death entered the world with the One (Jesus) who brings life. Again, we would have to say that Paul uses Adam only as a representative of the first humans.

On the other hand, it could be argued that this idea of more than two humans makes it easier to understand where Cain's wife came from and possibly who the 'sons of God' were in Genesis 6.

We have looked at the connection between Genesis and *biology*. But the question of the nature and origin of man comes within the scope of the science of *anthropology* too.

In several ways Genesis and anthropology are agreed. Genesis even foretells certain recent discoveries and ideas.

1. They are agreed on man's double nature – 'from dust, from God', as Bernard Ramm puts it. Although man is related in many ways to the animals, he is still distinct from them. He is able to analyse himself, know right and wrong, create works of art, and see his need of God.

2. They also agree in general that all mankind stems from one original race living in the region of Mesopotamia (that is, in the country we now call Syria, between the rivers Tigris and Euphrates).

These are remarkable similarities. But it doesn't mean we can look further into Genesis 3 and 4 for scientific detail. Nor can what is said there be proved by science.

We are told in Genesis that Adam and Eve lived in Eden until they disobeyed God. After this 'fall of man' (that is, Adam and Eve's disobedience), man was subject to death.

Some Christians would say that before the 'fall' all nature was 'perfect' in some sense. Physical death arose only when Adam disobeyed God.

Others believe that Eden was a limited area favourable to the life of man, and that outside it thistles, barren ground, storms and the rest of nature's hazards existed as they do today. We know, for example, from fossil records, that animals were dying long before man first dwelt on earth.

Science can't provide us with any evidence of man's life in Eden. There is little hope of finding today any evidence of less than a generation of blameless life lived so long ago.

But from other points of view there *is* direct evidence.

Our own minds show us a good which we can't attain. The whole of history traces the results of this 'fall'. It's no use saying that man has progressed a long way from savagery, or even from the wars of the middle ages, when only quite recently men, women and children have been herded into gas chambers and murdered in thousands.

In face of this, who can say that man is as God intended him to be?

As C. S. Lewis pointed out, we must not confuse 'primitive' with 'evil'. A being could be a savage in the sense that he was naked and unable to use a knife and fork. But he could still be so free from evil, so innocent, that we would be tempted to fall down and worship him.

Most anthropologists think that creatures physically resembling man existed as long as 500,000 years ago. Yet civilization is very young, dating from around 8000 BC. It is interesting that in the 500,000-year period so little evidence of physical change due to evolution can be seen.

Some theologians have been prepared to place Adam and Eve early in this period. Others believe that the very ancient fossils came from beings that were not men in the Bible sense, and that the change to 'living souls' came only about 10,000 years ago.

If this is so, then perhaps civilizations were the first obvious results of the 'fall'. It seems likely, at any rate, that some fundamental change in man's mental make-up took place near 8000 BC.

Genesis gives us some sort of dating in its genealogies, of course. But most scholars regard these as unsuitable for calculating dates, as they are not a sequence of strict father–son relationships. The genealogy of Jesus in Matthew is the same. Even the first readers must have recognized it as incomplete.

So what can we conclude about Genesis and science?

The Bible doesn't describe any process by which life was made. It simply states that God gave it existence.

The Bible shows that there was some sort of development over a period of time – the six 'days'.

Since Genesis isn't a scientific textbook it would be out of place to look there for detailed answers to purely scientific questions. And to do so would be to miss the deeper meaning of these chapters.

Augustine's commentary on the creation of Eve from Adam's rib is the most appropriate. He says she was taken not from his head to 'lord it over him', nor from his feet to be a servant, but from his side to be a companion.

The central fact of Genesis is God's formation of man in His own image.

Modern biology can in no way deny this.

8 Miracles

There comes a moment when people
who have been dabbling in religion
('Man's search for God' !) suddenly
draw back. Supposing we really found
Him? We never meant it to come to
that. Worse still, supposing He had
found us?

So it is a sort of Rubicon. One goes
across; or not. But if one does, there
is no manner of security against
miracles —
C. S. Lewis.

It isn't easy to define the word 'miracle'. We use it rather
loosely today. We talk about a 'miraculous' recovery from
an illness. We say of a friend's ancient car: 'It's a miracle it
goes at all.'

On the whole we tend to use the word to mean 'wonderful'
or 'extraordinary'. We certainly don't always mean to imply
that God's hand is at work.

**The unusual events in the Bible which we call
miracles are understood by the biblical writers as
'signs' that God is working in a special way, inter-
rupting the ordinary course of things.**

The Bible's miracles aren't all of the same type. The
Gospels describe those performed by Christ when He was
on earth. Others, described in Acts, are connected with the
young Christian church. Or there are the miracles in the
Old Testament involving the prophets who led the Jews
at various stages of their turbulent history.

What are we to make of the Bible's miracles today?

The central miracle of Christianity is Christ's incarnation – the Son of God becoming a human being. If Christ is God, surely we would expect unusual events to take place during His life on earth?

'The Word became flesh and dwelt among us' is how the apostle John put it. But long before this happened, the Jewish prophet Isaiah wrote of a baby who would be called 'Emmanuel', 'God with us'.

Christ referred many times to His own deity. The great Jewish expression used by God of His own existence was 'I am'. (See Exodus 3:13, 14, for example.) Jesus said of Himself, 'Before Abraham was born, "I Am".'

In view of these statements, it is impossible to regard Jesus merely as a teacher of morals. But many people, who don't know the Gospels very well, hold this view.

As C. S. Lewis said, 'A man who was merely a man and said the sort of things Jesus said wouldn't be a great moral teacher. He'd either be a lunatic – on a level with a man who says he's a poached egg – or else he'd be the Devil of Hell. You must make your choice. Either this man was, and is, the Son of God: or else a madman or something worse. . . . But don't let us come with any patronizing nonsense about His being a great human teacher. He hasn't left that open to us. He didn't intend to.'*

Granted this central fact, that Christ is God's Son, author of all life, of course He would be able to heal the sick or raise the dead!

For many of its 'miracles' the Bible itself supplies a natural explanation – that is, an explanation in terms of the forces usually at work in the world of nature.

This is the case in Moses' crossing of the Red Sea (already mentioned in chapter 4). A strong east wind is said to have driven the sea back (look up Exodus 14:21).

The miracle here is the timing. An unbelieving person would say that it was simply an amazing coincidence that

* *Broadcast Talks* (Geoffrey Bles).

the wind blew back the waters just as Moses and the Israelites turned up.

The same could be said of Elijah's demonstration on Mount Carmel (see 1 Kings 18). Some people would say that it was most fortunate that a thunderbolt or something came down and lit the altar fire just after Elijah had prayed that God would reveal His power.

But there comes a point when it is easier to come to the conclusion that God answered the prayers of such men than that a series of fantastic coincidences occurred. It is the same with the so-called 'explanations' of Christ's resurrection:

We are told that He wasn't really dead, in spite of all the wounds He received and the hours on that terrible gallows.

Or that His body was stolen when the Jews had put on a special guard to prevent that very thing.

Or that those who saw the risen Jesus were all having hallucinations, or mass hysteria in the case of the 500 who saw Him all at once.

It is easier to accept the fact that God raised His Son from the dead than to believe all the far-fetched 'explanations'. Without the resurrection, we can't explain the sudden change in the disciples' behaviour, either. They had been men hiding behind barred doors for fear of the Jews. But they became preachers in the very synagogues themselves, men who 'turned the world upside down'.

There would be no church today if it hadn't been for that change – and the event which caused it.

Some people have felt that science rules miracles 'out of court' as impossible events. But it isn't true to say that science excludes the possibility of miracles.

Now, some things are impossible in the sense of being self-contradictory – for instance, that two and two should make five or that a body should fail to move when impelled by an irresistible force. These statements are impossible because of our definitions of 'two' and 'irresistible', in the same way that black can't be white.

But this isn't the sort of impossibility that these people have in mind. They say that the laws of science actually *forbid* miracles.

But we saw in chapter 5 that the laws of science don't *cause* anything. So they can't *forbid* anything. They are just descriptions of what actually happens.

We also saw in that chapter that we can't *prove* that nature is uniform, however many observations we make. We just have to assume it. So we can't say that things are impossible because they seem to 'go against nature'.

In the Christian view, God is responsible for the ordinary happenings of nature. When a miracle takes place it is because He injects a new factor into the situation. We are not saying that in miracles nature suddenly does things for no reason. Miracles are unusual events caused by God.

So if scientists can't prove that miracles are impossible, they can at least ask whether the records of miracles are historically accurate.

We have better documents for the Bible miracles than for events such as the Roman invasion of Britain which everyone believes in!

In some cases there is archaeological evidence too.

One reason why certain early documents, such as the Apocryphal Gospels, weren't included when the Bible was given its final form, was that they were full of rather pointless miracles.

The Bible's miracles are quite different. They show that God is interested in right and wrong, in healing people or feeding them. They are neither propaganda nor magic.

We tend to say that miracles couldn't happen because we aren't used to them! This doesn't prove anything.

In a sense, everything is incredible. It is amazing that trees should burst into leaf once a year, or that the earth should spin in empty space, or that one small cell should grow into a man.

We stop marvelling because we are so used to it all. But someone from a world where such things were unknown might be excused if he said 'impossible' when he heard of them.

Strictly speaking, it is no more incredible that God should cause a virgin to conceive a child twenty centuries ago in Galilee than that He should cause the earth to produce its first germ of life in prehistoric times.

But is it reasonable that there should be miracles? We have seen that science doesn't exclude the possibility. Are they just pointless examples of God's power, or part of some long-term plan?

The Bible suggests that miracles are essential parts of God's plan to save the human race from evil.

God's chosen people were to keep pure their knowledge of God until 'the right time', when His own Son should be born as a man and eventually be put to death for the sins of the whole world. This may seem a strange remedy for the world's ills, to human ears! But the message of this gospel, accepted by individual men and women, has made changes in hearts and lives which are often miraculous too.

On miracles, as on the other issues raised in earlier chapters, science is neutral. It neither affirms nor denies the truth of the Bible. Its whole method of approach and terms of reference aren't appropriate for such a judgment.

9 Essentials

It is their faint hearts rather than their
brilliant heads that stand between
them and Christ –
Billy Graham.

'Well, what of it?' asks the agnostic reader.

'Let's be generous and grant that this science versus the
Bible conflict is mythical after all. So what next? The Bible
might have been all right for primitive people, but *we* live in a
scientific age. Far better to send one good agriculturalist or
doctor to so-called "heathen" countries than any number of
missionaries!'

'The same goes for Britain. If we're to survive, we've got
to have more research men in industry and better nuclear
power generators. These are what matters – not the Bible.'

You often hear this sort of criticism. In trying to answer
it, let's imagine what sort of impression our world might
make on a complete stranger, say a Martian, who had
travelled widely with good interpreters.

What would he find?

A strange world where less than half the inhabitants live
in great comfort with many scientific discoveries to help
them, while the rest live in want.

Only a small minority of the people in the rich nations try
to help the others. The rest are indifferent. They have even

been known to burn their extra food so that prices will stay high, instead of sending it to the nations that are starving.

Most of the rich countries, the Martian would discover, spend vast sums of money each year on machines which can destroy men and cities. But they spend very little on building hospitals or finding out new things to help mankind.

True, he would see good men all over the world living innocent lives with their families. But most men would seem like islands in a sea of self-interest. Unless some great calamity draws them together, they aren't even concerned with their neighbours, let alone those half a world away.

If the Martian went to hear what the leaders of the rich nations had to say, he would find them asking for more scientists, which often seems to mean thinking up more ways of making death for other men.

But he would see that although those who have the most of this science live in comfort, they aren't much happier than the rest of the world. And they still have fear in their hearts.

Science doesn't make people good either, he would see. Those who have it do as many harmful things as the others. The only difference is that those with the science can harm more quickly and more deeply.

The visitor might well come to the conclusion that the men and women in the world need new hearts – not new power or knowledge. So the only question worth asking is how to find these 'new hearts'.

Unless people down the centuries have been very much mistaken, the New Testament offers that very thing.

To find out about the Christian faith, we need to look at the evidence for ourselves.

Not many people bother to do that. Some of us still have the vague ideas that we picked up as children, or on an occasional trip to church. Or we have rejected the whole thing without giving it any thought, just because our friends don't bother with it (maybe they haven't thought either!).

Are we sure what Christianity is all about? Have we taken

the trouble to look out the evidence? This is the *scientific* way of doing things after all.

There's no shortage of books about the Christian faith, written from every possible viewpoint. Best of all, there is the Bible itself. Anyone reading the Gospels, the Acts and the New Testament Letters is bound to be impressed by the sincerity of the writers, to say the very least!

But it isn't just a question of finding out the evidence. Christianity involves a choice.

There is a line to be crossed. Although nearly rubbed out by many of today's writers and preachers, it stands clear in Christ's own words: 'Anyone who is not for me is really against me.' Or in John's: 'Whoever has the Son has (eternal) life.'

Don't let us imagine we'll be carried to heaven with the crowd. The crowd isn't going that way, as far as one can judge!

A choice has to be made before the line is crossed. The cost may be heavy, once the choice is made.

An honest reader of the Gospels has to decide whether they are beautiful fairy stories, or the most tremendous news the world can offer. It's a solemn decision.

What is the tremendous news, then? Briefly, that God's own Son died on a common gallows so that all men might be forgiven and live for ever.

The idea that we need to be sorry for what we have done, and be forgiven, is foreign to us in this scientific age. It's always so much easier to see the faults of relatives and friends than our own.

But there is selfishness in everyone. Given favourable conditions, this grows into the things which fill our newspapers with such depressing reading.

The Bible's message is that only God can deliver us from this and make new men and women out of us.

Nothing will put right the world's troubles – except a new quality of life.

Today nearly all politicians the world over are aiming for more scientific progress. But in the long run science isn't what is going to matter most. It is individual men who matter.

Atomic power has to be controlled by men.

Good or bad men.

Men interested in their own comfort, their own power.

Or men willing to love God and their fellow-men more than anything else.

Political systems, however just, aren't going to cure the world of sin. In fact, they all depend on good men for their success.

Complicated codes of morals or of laws are powerless too. Only a new quality of life will do, and this is what the Christian gospel offers.

Jesus said to Nicodemus, a clever man and a deeply religious one, 'Do not be surprised because I tell you, "You must all be born again." ' Summarizing the facts about Christ, a New Testament letter says: 'God has given us eternal life, and this life is ours in his Son. Whoever has the Son has this life; whoever does not have the Son of God does not have life.'

Appropriately, the only way to check the truth of this is the scientific one. We need to make the experiment, to put our trust in the Person who is so clearly portrayed in the Gospel narratives.

The first step may be to read one of these Gospels in a modern version. Sometimes learning may be a hindrance, whether scientific or not. The apostle Peter, in his simple, down-to-earth way, came to the heart of the matter. 'Lord, to whom would we go? You have the words that give eternal life.'

Further reading

A book like this, written primarily for students, can't be more than an introduction. For those who want to go further into the subject, there is no shortage of books on science and Christianity! As I can't list them all, I am going to mention the few that helped me most. Some of these are on more general topics.

Those which I found best of all were written by C. S. Lewis, who wasn't a scientist or a theologian! They include *Mere Christianity*, *The Screwtape Letters*, *The Abolition of Man* and *Miracles*.

The only criticism I have is with *Miracles*. I think the argument of the earlier chapters would be better if the whole of nature was taken to be directly dependent on the Creator, instead of only parts of it, such as our thought processes.

That Hideous Strength, also by C. S. Lewis (in his own words a 'tall story' about devilry), deals excitingly with the ruthless exploitation of scientific discovery. It is published by The Bodley Head or in paperback by Pan Books.

The others were originally published by Geoffrey Bles.

Miracles, The Screwtape Letters and *Mere Christianity* are available as Fontana paperbacks.

The following books, written from differing viewpoints, will be useful for study. They may contradict one another, but you learn more from seeing both sides of a question.

E. L. Mascall, *Christian Theology and Natural Science* (Longmans, 1956).

B. Ramm, *The Christian View of Science and Scripture* (Paternoster Press, 1955).

Richard Acworth, *Creation, Evolution and the Christian Faith* (Evangelical Press, 1969).

R. E. D. Clark, *Darwin, Before and After* (Paternoster Press, 1948).

A. F. Smethurst, *Modern Science and Christian Belief* (Nisbet, 1955).

C. E. Raven, *Natural Religion and Christian Theology*, vols. 1 and 2 (Cambridge University Press, 1953).

F. F. Bruce, *The New Testament Documents: Are They Reliable?* (Inter-Varsity Press, 5th ed., 1970).

Malcolm A. Jeeves, *The Scientific Enterprise and Christian Faith* (Tyndale Press, 1969).

Finally, for those who want an authoritative textbook, *Issues in Science and Religion* by I. G. Barbour (SCM Press, 1966) provides a very full and balanced account of the whole subject. It has plenty of further references and is more readable than most textbooks.